Contents

Introduction

When the writing workshop began at Eastern Correctional Facility of New York (also known as Napanoch) three years ago, none of us had any idea it would assume a life of its own. I was invited by a professor in what was then a college course, to come in and do a class on poetry. It was a smashing success. I took advantage of the enthusiasm by volunteering to run a series of workshops at night, when the school was in session. Thanks to the enlightened administration of Superintendent David Miller, Deputy Superintendent of Programs Cheryl Butler, Volunteer Services Coordinator Charles Piera, and Head Librarian Pauline Lewis, the idea became reality.

The handful of writers and I were given a tiny room off the main library, with a door that separated us from the general population. To come through the door, all that was required was a pencil, paper, and the desire to write. If you didn't have pencil or paper, we could lend you some. But the desire to write had to be your own.

About this time, the terrible Presidential decision to eliminate all federal Pell Grants for college education in prisons took effect. The one sure tool for positive change inside each student/prisoner had been taken away; the one proven method in practically eliminating recidivism had been abandoned; the expectation that the student body in American prisons would be able to put their talent, intelligence, and energy to work upon re-entering society had been cut off at the roots. The student body at Eastern, several members of which were in our workshop, responded by becoming teachers themselves, tutoring those who'd had little or no education to achieve literacy, get a GED diploma, and prepare for college entrance exams, should they ever again be offered.

Meanwhile, our workshop gave its first poetry reading for the general population. It happened on a full moon night in September. We called it **Voices Under the Harvest Moon.** A film crew from Deep Dish TV taped the performance, which drew in new talent from the audience. We decided to call ourselves **The Harvest Moon Collective.**

What has been remarkable from the beginning is the dedication the writers have brought to the sessions. With a revolving leadership and shared decision-making no one gets bogged down in their own ideas for too long. Every talent is employed for the benefit of all, and once a week each one of us has at least these three hours to write. A groundwork of trust and the expectation we have for each other's new work has created a momentum— a shared consciousness and exchange of ideas that gallops along. Each participant is teaching, inspiring and critiquing himself, as well as everyone else. The leap in growth in the individual writers has been astounding. For me it has been the springboard to much of the new writing I've been doing. The anthology in your hands is three years worth of writers who, despite the confines of time and space, have carved out their own voices.

One evening in the first year of our workshop, someone came through the door to select a videotape from the stack kept in a cupboard in the corner. Our circle was in the midst of an animated discussion. Since all talk inside the room was private, I looked up at the man who had his back to us, and was still looking in the cupboard. One by one the men stopped speaking. How long does it take to choose a tape? Obviously our visitor wanted to know what we were doing. But he had come through the door without the required implements. I stopped talking, too. Without a word, or turning to face us, the man left. None of us spoke. In a few minutes, he came back in, and left again. Our space felt violated. I wrote a poem. It was done as an acrostic.

Which Side Are You On?

Where does my anger come from
        at the laziness, the prosaic?
How many times will you enter a room
        and leave it vacant: in and out,
in and out, visiting a temple of possibility
        and never leave a gift on the altar?

Come down to the river of your own soul, we are
        excavating
here, the yellow helmets you see are so many
suns on the horizon, going down and coming up
in no particular time sequence or order.

When one flower opens, Kabir says,
                    ordinarily
dozens open. I'm digressing.

Every time you visit yourself without
                    respect, you lose. Without love,
Also.
Read the coins you've thrown down into the dirt,
                    they spell *integrity.* You recall those
early moments in
your young life when you sang. And we were
                    witnesses—if not then, now. We can
                              see you
outside the ordinary, grab onto a miracle and
understand it was no more you than the wind.

Oh, so that's it, finally.
No more you or me than that mountain
                    there. And no mountain either.
                              Which side are you on?

In a society that loves to cast blame but does not like to assume responsibility for conditions we have created or allowed to exist, perhaps we need to ask ourselves the same question. Are we for growth or condemnation? Are we for sharing, or remaining isolated in our own cells, wherever they are? In the struggle to make this world a place we like to live in, which side are we on?

— *Janine Pommy Vega*

Frank Fissette

A Letter of Intention

I got another letter from your mother today, Paddy.
A picture of your entire family dated 1962 and "one of the last
of the happy times," written on the back.
She wants to hear again about how good you did in college and
tells me how sorry she is she missed your graduation.
I told her (again) about your excellent grades and how proud she
would have been seeing you get your diploma, even though you
only finished two semesters.
She told me how happy she was that you didn't use drugs and I
agreed you were the smartest kid in your neighborhood when
it came to dope, while I thought about the money we spent
together putting some connection's son through law school.
She told me again how you never had a chance, and how you were
always getting into trouble over other people.
I said some of us just don't have any luck and it's all in the
roll of the dice, but I never once mentioned the word ringleader.
She even wrote about your faith in God, and how often you went to
church, and I laughed hysterically without saying a word about
how much you hated priests and their Christian dogma.
One son lost on a dirt road in the Vietnamese countryside.
One on the filthy streets of New York City.
Another who turned ten to twenty years into a life sentence.
I have no right to receive her letters.
I have no right to tell her lies.
I have no right to tell her the truth.
When I see you again, whether it's up there or down there,
you're getting a black eye.
I now have that right.

Dreams of Life

He lies on a bed of cold steel on an inch thick mattress at three-thirty in the morning, trying to see through the bars on his window and the wall that's his only view, and chants over and over again, I will not cry, I will not cry, as he dreams of the things he misses.

He misses rose bushes, daffodils, tulips in the spring, lilacs in the summer, the smell of pines and the shade of maples, fields of corn, poison ivy, weed-choked lots, thorn bushes, stinkweed, and gardens where nothing grows.

I will not cry. I will not cry.

He misses dogs with cold noses and wagging tails, playful kittens, whistling songbirds, fish tanks filled with every color of the rainbow, deer grazing in a field, rats feeding on huge piles of stinking garbage, mice in the empty cupboards, cockroaches on the kitchen ceiling, pigeons and snakes.

I will not cry. I will not cry.

He misses babies laughing, children playing tag, beautiful girls in cut-off jeans, old people who tell their stories, parades, smelly old winos, obnoxious panhandlers, drug dealers, pimps, gangs, and crowds of surly strangers.

I will not cry. I will not cry.

He misses his mother, brothers, sisters, grandfather, and favorite old aunt, the father he never knew, the cousin who stabbed him, the uncle who testified against him, and the friends he never had.

I will not cry. I will not cry.
He misses having something to look forward to, the sense of
belonging some place, dreams, caring, loving, empathy, self-

respect, appreciating life, and hope.

I will not cry. I will not cry. I cannot cry any more.

Let The Punishment Fit The Crime

Seeing that little girl lying there in that box
all I can think of is you.
Her smile is gone.
Her laugh,
Her serious answers to silly questions,
her complete trust in anyone grown up,
all gone.
All because of you.
I don't want you all gone though.
I don't want you electrocuted,
injected, strung up or shot down.
I want you to live forever
in that stinking prison
where the best of the worst make your every moment
on this planet miserable, painful, and worse torture
than any inquisition ever offered.
I want you to suffer like you made me suffer
by making her suffer.
Don't die by the hand of the state, child killer.
Live in pain.

Final Performance

Big heavy oaken doors that must weigh two tons apiece
open up a huge chamber full of long wooden benches
kept polished and shiny by the pants seats
of the true believers
and lifeless hypocrites.
Walnut paneling, dropped ceilings, and plush red carpets
muffle the sounds of the performers inside.
Tables piled high with thick leather books
that are open for interpretation.
Dead center, high above everyone else,
seated at the altar,
a man in flowing black robes
plays to a packed house.
My co-star.
A baby cries,
but not for me.
Family members,
not mine,
are lending moral support.
They claim to be followers of Christ
but demand Old Testament justice.
The foul breath of my assistant
reeks of moldy money
as he whispers, "Show some respect if you have something to say."
"Fuck you," I tell him.
My co-star peers over his glasses at me,
(they always peer over their glasses)
and starts rattling off my credits.
An encore would be nice.
Finally he asks for my speech.
With precious few seconds to deliver, I improvise and give the same

speech I gave my assistant.
Finally, time for my award.
My co-star smiled as he gave me life.
The critics made a big deal out of my smiling back at him.

They don't realize that all I really got
was something I already took,
and something I never had.
Bravo.

Don't Believe Everything You Hear

Hey porcupine,
I heard you stink!
Don't worry about it, because I heard it from a poet and a prisoner,
both traditionally unreliable sources.
Naturally I had to find out for myself.
None of the books I read said a word about how you smell
but they did call you a rodent.
That's all right too, though, since all the books that haven't been
burned are also traditionally unreliable.
I'd like to find out, one way or the other, if you smell more than
most humans,
so come out of hiding and meet me in a parking lot some place
because I'm not about to meet you on your own ground.
You carry too many knives on your back,
and as we both know
Knives are traditionally reliable.

Fugitive

Fleeing across country in a pair of beat-up old wingtips stolen
from a back porch that was a little too close to the prison to be
worried about thieves and other men of honor.

Upstanding citizens screaming for my head. A head that's losing
hair, lumpy, and empty of any concern for their health, wealth, and
welfare. Another head to stuff and put over their bars and admire
as they drink their whiskey and beer.

Gin martinis and smoking jackets are what I crave right now. Silk
ascots embroidered with my initials —F.T.W.— in each corner, and
razor blade slippers to remind me of the joy of my youth.

Icebergs are warmer than my thoughts of home. I have no home to run
to anymore, but as long as I keep on running I'll always have
some place to go. Never stop. Never rest. Never give up.

Taste the difference in the air. The rain, the mud, the sweat all
taste better when there's no wall around them. Walls taste like hair
loaded down with so much pomade you keep slipping behind them.
Further and further away from wanting to be free.

Idle hands really are the devil's workshop. They have nothing to do
so they chase me. Keep coming, demon boys, because today I'm a god.
A Viking warrior god. Meaner than Odin and better looking than Thor.
A whole lot smarter than you and a whole lot more appreciative
and aware of what I don't have.

Vacancy should be the sign hanging outside my cage right about now.
I'm not letting you bring me back. This is war and in war there are

no rules. Do you want to be a hero? Die in the service of your government? It will be much more peaceful for the both of us if you just go ahead and rent the room to someone else willing to stay a while. Someone willing to believe he's as bad as you tell him he is.

Elope is a synonym for escape. I've run away to get married to the me you introduced me to. I sure wish I had a better pair of shoes.

Jeff Lowery

Mountaineering

In the mountains you dream of the real
world. Every day you wake up. You're in the street.

You must be strong, believe in yourself, or
nobody will. You won't survive.

Slowly weaving spiders will ensnare your humanity,
injecting numbing venom through hollow fangs into
a tattering caricature, dissolving segment by
segment into the foundation of the web.

Every day you wake yourself, dream of the mountains,
create the real world, despise the streets; pretend
you survive.

HABIB

The candle of your aura draws me through the corridor
of despair like
Percival to the well.
Gently it fans a spark insulated in layers of ash
to a flickering tendril of flame.
For a moment we bask in the glory of a jewel that has
known few others, cupped in loving hands.
CIAO!
Fate decrees we experience our humanity fleetingly.
The jewel swaddled away from the reality
that bows our spirits like

stunted pines above the timber line.
We spar comically
You jabbing at the man's man,
Me hooking at the sensitive male:
Two moths circling the same flame.

Milkweed Seed

Pacing the cage in F-2,
the S.H.U. in Comstock for the uninitiated,
jail for the jailed,
I'm absently rubbing the handcuff welts
on my wrists, concentrating on calming
the rage lashing through me like a stalking
tiger's tail. I'm attempting to close
the hole in my soul slashed by my accepting
dehumanization again.

The Con, down 12, hard. A chrysalis
of self-hatred is ripped from the cocoon by
... a milkweed seed?
It floats through the bars on a vagrant
gust of wind. Its gossamer threads
a frozen white hot explosion, the radii
slender conduits to past and future life.

As the seed settles weightlessly
in my palm, I watch my daughter
through tears that wash into my smile,
a child once again, I pluck a ripe
pod from the stalk and laughing
scatter wishes into the wind.

View from The Crow's Nest

Exploring my childhood creek
searching the continuum of time for a link
in the chain of existence, I'm surprised
the water splashing against the moss splotched
boulders beneath my feet no longer conjures
pirate ships. Intently I scan the wind
for my father's voice.

Cunningly, the sound of the wind
focuses me, as it channels through exposed
roots of a toppled wild cherry bridging
the creek banks, its taproot refusing
to release its grip on solid ground.

Is that his voice in the channeled wind,
or the silver curtains of minnows flashing
from bank to bank as my shadow falls
on the water? Could it be the golden winged
pair of dragonflies flirting with their
reflections on the water's surface?

Gazing through nature's crystal,
minnows, wind, dragonflies, and the sound
of running water meld like dots in a Monet.
A lazy hazy summer sun shines on wild
flowers and grasses. Black Irish blue eyes
warm my shoulders. Once again sea dogs
armed with wooden swords prepare to
repel the boarders from moss splotched decks.

Daido

Is brea liom sean-fhear. I know that's enough, but I'm sharing
this with friends, and they need a bigger picture.
Never will forget them telling you not to teach us to speak,
that this is America.
Only in the last eleven years have I understood the pain
you must have felt. You passed the flame well. The Martyrs of '16
live within me.
Crucible where I was poured, veil of childhood nurtured,
armor of manhood tempered and forged. Nucleus for the child
you cherished, man now at war.
You wrote that. I know you understand it, too, just as I feel
your energy brighten as I send this vibration.
Hours spent in your lap, enveloped by your love, mesmerized
by the images your voice created: heroes and villains
you invoked and made perform in *seanmh'athair's* sanctuary,
her gods looking askance.
"Gertie, 'tis me house, woman, give the *by* the glassful."
Those hours weren't wasted. The seeds you planted
fluoresce in my love for the written and spoken word, for the
treasures revealed, for the surreal reality of a master's
brush strokes, the sun's sublime imagery as it rises and sets,
children's laughter, the sparkle in a happy woman's eye.
The warmth of your smile as I told your grandson's mother,
"His name's Kevin Barry, or he's no son of mine,"
still radiates from my skin. The laughter
I just heard will always deliver an arrow, and the echo
of an empty shell.
The *spaleen* no longer *belabors the par harse.* Matter of fact,
don't hurt animals at all any more. Still revere rocks, though.
The ones that speak tease me occasionally, reminding me how they
used to get my ass whipped by the shillelagh you wielded so well.

Took a while, but I now know it truly was administered,
to steal a line, "in the name of love."

Three things before I go.
First, were we really redeemed when I billy conned Danny Muldoon?
Yeah, I know he split my eyebrow. Three years and fifteen pounds
is a reasonable handicap, *sean-fhear*.
Besides, he whipped your Russell a few weeks before,
and the old lady distracted me.
Second, why didn't you tell me, when your aura drew me back
and back again to the coffin, and later when it sparkled over
Gram sleeping, that you were loving her and nowhere close to gone?
Lastly, because one of your many gifts was a twisted sense
of humor, does our Trudie run the sphere youse share
like she did your house?

Daido: Grandfather in Gaelic
Is brea liom sean-fhear: I love you, old man
Seanmhathair: Grandmother

19

Big Apple Minutiae

Death on the edge of town
Manic traffic
Kisses by the water line
Polaroid
Someone goes to fetch the party's host
Central Park
Pigeons cooing after melba toast
Hobos benching
Somewhere an eight-figure deal is struck
Rock Cafe—celebrity beehive
Pretty woman in a zoot suit tries her luck
Hale applause, major cause:
Sex change wriggling on the dance floor
Someone's crying. Loan denied. Try again
Working spies, poker eyes
Everyone is getting a new name
Life goes on, fake it or not
Jogger's high, cardiac blare
Somewhere a child wishes she could vote
Trousers down, hair undone
Prices up like mayoral balloons
Fad goes out (boxer whipped);
Enter Beasty Spike
Competition, take a hike:
Wonder Boy has built a thinner chip
Black girl fuming: hubby tried
What good is it if you're not there
When baby counts to ten?

The Fossils of Your Mind

Pressed up in folds of circumstance
And metamorphic dreams
They bear the frowns of change to tell
The story of your life
Like forests petrified
Imprinted faces grin like shells in sedimentary rock
Your broken arm
That Sunday dress
Your first attempt at love
They're moths, footprints and trilobites
In your memorial soil.

Your bones will go the way of seeping rain
And ancient dinosaurs
When you will put to rest for good
Your quaternary doubts
But every verse that's written
In the scrolls of your soul
Will follow trails of fleeting reveries
On wings of dragonflies.

The Seven Planes of The Explorer

The first plane of the explorer is
The microcosm of fallopian bliss
A world of perfect harmony
Ruled only by the clock of expectation
Of the million man swim
Across the Joy Canal—

The second plane of the explorer is
The womb proper
His dream machine
For traveling without cause and effect
He would rather not leave it
But the pattern of chaos is on
And he must exit to a play
Which begins with cries.

The third plane of the explorer is the cradle
Safe and comfortable
Although less than before
Because sooner or later he must take his first step
Which will be his first fall also

On his fourth plane
He discovers a place he calls home
Which feels like the cosmos
But shrinks inevitably with time
As it pushes him toward the boundary of adolescent disorder
Torn again between the known and the unknown
He knows he must go on

Now he faces a world they call
The real world
And wonders what was wrong with the other ones
In time the explorer questions
The reality and stability of the fifth plane

And gets a longing for the stars—

On his sixth plane
The explorer takes off
He jumps, he flies, and sometimes he even leaves the earth
For days at a time in a space shuttle
Or in a drug-induced euphoria

And then before he knows it
He is over the edge
And discovers that he is about to leave for good
Never knowing what awaits him

On the seventh plane
He only knows that change is constant
And knowing this law
He takes the dreaded step
On wings of chance and circumstance.

The Alcove

I remember J Street, we used to hang out
in the alcove, the front of the cafe,
it was shaped like an M.
Poetry was our life. That's all we did.
Kids of the street, that's all
we did was poetry.
The alcove was our home.
There was another Shawn. He was always
so spiritual. Every day he talked about
something new that he'd learned.
He loved books. He always had a book.
The Satanic Bible, Arts & Weaponry.
He was tall, black hair, pale skin,
wore a bandanna on his head.
We'd sit on the floor, drink sodas,
we'd read to each other.
I was fifteen.
On certain nights they had open mic.
That's when I wrote The Wondering Soul,
I had a tape recorder, and taped it
as it came to me. I probably stopped
so many times that the button wore out.

Moon

Looking back at my shadow, my thoughts require patience.
It seems bent in a stride unwelcome to company.
It looks too mocked.
I think about my long dead dog,
He used to follow me and race after my shadow as I walked
in the moonlight.

Tonight the moon seems to be fading. It looks like a fine
bright hole arranging sympathy for those of us who wander
in a life of decorated controversy. Misunderstood
at this moment, I feel like a clown obtaining trust.

I remember my parents telling me there was a man in the moon.
Often I looked up and wished I could tell that person
a thing or two.
Tonight I wish to snatch that grin off and place it
beside my dog who died defending me a long time ago.

My shadow moves to one side, then the other.
Often it moves alongside me, then runs off in front
of my pace. No wonder my dog chased it.
It trades places so often.

On My Way

At a very young age I found being a step-child had a range
of feelings unsuitable for concern.
People looked at me, but really unconcerned.
I chewed what hurt the most, and felt unjustly cursed.
That was the critical role with the rural reflections controlling
my happiness.
A happiness clawed by doubt.
I composed a plaintive cry without sound,
an ache that was rendered inexpedient.

My quiet moments had a hypnotic effect
I felt like a nearby person looking at a different life
a mere mile away, where the newer undignified friends
swooped much farther ahead.
My child life gradually became less visible,
it deliciously dropped,
landing somewhere without bending, or scattering
any unbearable value.

Being a little poor conspicuous figure with a synthetic mind
and aged well beyond my already frightened life,
I wanted to cry openly, but my emotions
were out of tune with the love that was really needed.
That left me pacing without moving.
I felt inarticulate and a stranger to myself.
I wanted to scale opportunity, and make a change
one would appreciate
because my faith was so ultimately outweighed.

On my own I felt despair at an eyebrow raising answer
to a soft unprecedented question.

And right there I left my rainbow behind me.
Right where it began dropping so deliciously.

Longing Blues   I

Last week I watched a man describing satisfaction
in a lengthening execution.
Shaken beyond sympathy, I felt
curled up inside a curious phenomenon,
encouraged to face the obedience in false moments:
the effect of remaining, knowing it will be of no avail.
I wanted to brush aside the curtain of intrusion
so freedom could be seen in the near distance.

I knew people could deal with respect for the blues
and reign behind a door forcibly shut.

A few days afterwards I watched him
dealing with whatever was usual, without announcing
sorrow which is already forfeit.
He moved without listening to what has taken over.
He walked simmering the journey in a manner unpoisoned,
facing the daily lock-back full of contentment and promise.

Last week I watched four busy fingers dating six strings
with sweet influence, from a melody eternal,
beautiful chords not played from a misery composition.
He looked so peaceful,
unshown stress taking him up, covering the debt,
The movement of music bringing him down in the anxiety of freedom,
notes bringing inspection of joy
swelling louder.

He awoke a thirst for the prescription for life, and a bond
to stop any leak from freedom of the mind,
as we awake to absent things.

Dear Loved One

It's been four days since my departure.
My sharp division of cowardice engineered me to write
you this while camouflaged somewhere.
I truly adored your warmth.
Instead of confronting you and preserving integrity
I left imagining you understood the friendship
in my most treasured feeling about you.
Now I feel empty, my imagination thwarted, I lean
nourishing and etching your unique signature.
My bones are very sturdy because of your special care.

You stroke my memory. I keep blending the softer hues
of your truth, that glowing love you let me explore.
You make me feel like an artist with an alien sense,
where passion arises only from an eye-watering
masterpiece, one intentionally felt and privately
needed to match the mind's conception.
So far, each day, you have repeatedly thrilled me
without holding hands or kissing privately,
with a tender violence pending.

Even at this astounding early distance those memories
curtail the Alpha of my progress from staying
so completely away.
Before boarding the Greyhound bus my heart pushed
against my lungs. I panted as I stood and thought

about truly leaving your body, so rigid with joy.
Your companionship is so pleasingly secret.
I watched the parading fumes from the diesel fuel
twirl in the night's cool air. I felt blindfolded inside
your passionate echoes, so rich inside my body, the lavish
sensation distributed by your strict way of pleasing me.

After boarding the bus and settling in the seat, as the wheels
carried me further into another reason for paved soil,
an unfair surprise of loneliness rushed me.
I wished for you.

My moment felt so terribly tender,
only your body's fragrance could lift me, viewing
your soft happy eyes.
Hopefully my leaving won't rattle that image of me
too pitifully. Because I love you professionally,
but doing for you properly falls before me, and you are
too wonderful to want anything cornucopially.

I kneel like a leaf that fell from a tree contemplating
breathing room. I spawn a silent redundant tear,
undressing my pride.
My cowardice contains the seeds of inadvertence.
After reading this, please open the door.
Your love shall not be disputed.
For I left my key,
and I might knock too hard.
I am flaming for you.

Seven

A few months ago, we as a group awaited an answer
from the Senate leader who proclaimed
that the officer who'd shot all seven
nine year old boys was justified
because one of the youngsters swung and aimed a toy gun at him.

A special Attorney General investigation
was in heated session.
That afternoon the Grand Jury ruled
the officer acted in accord with his training.

Afterwards, I hung my head and felt so unusual.
Later that night I got arrested for being too drunk in public
while just looking up at the vast night sky, amazed.

I awoke later in the bull pen
with the officer who was cleared of the killings.
He was arrested for being too frightened
to be alone and still.

Peekaboo

Peekaboo. I see you. I have seen you.
I saw you standing in the eyes of the sands of time.
Peekaboo. I saw you standing,
writhing as they tried to wipe the black off my hide.
And when I did not cry out in pain, they wiped
me harder. Peekaboo.
I stared into your eyes scheming for the truth
and the reason why, only to find the true love
you have for me and my kind.
And then I thought, Who are you? Who am I to you?
Nothing but a microscopic particle
off a speck that has been riding on the waves of vapors,
off the moisture of a raindrop that has fallen
up on a leaf in a rain forest, where it has been
raining for a billion years. Peekaboo.
I who am nobody to everybody in time, I am that
particle that once was a proud king, who ruled over
a land of proud and beautiful people.
To them time was everything, and everything was time.
Peekaboo. I saw you watching my spirit as we
traveled down through time, and you were
wondering then, Who am I?
I'm but the first rays of the morning sun that fall
upon the flowers in your garden. They open up,
willing to be raped by the bees making honey.
Peekaboo. What am I but the fingers on the hands
of the young lady who sits alone in the dark,
who is longing for love, but has no one to love,
as I, those fingers, move slowly and gently

across her breast, moving down to the mounted
love between her legs for a joyful reunion of love
and lust. Peekaboo. Do you see who I am?
I'm that sweet talking big black man
who your mother tried to warn your sisters about,
the kind that she could not get enough of herself.

I saw her watching me out of the corner
of my eye as I passed by, pretending to turn
her nose up at me, when all the time she was only
trying to get a glance of my scent out of the air.
How intoxicating ambrosia could be the fruit
of the Gods, which I am. You see? Peekaboo.
I am but love for all.

Hidden Passion

Bastille, the secrets of one's heart and soul.
Let the singing of her fourth wing sting the man-child within.
Step forward with the passion to accept the wind
from her fourth wing. To be baptized with the virtue
of her lust from the forgotten alleys of her heart,
and accept the wire-like turbulence
that is her lust for love.
It is a gift that was given to you from the god Aeulus,
the king of Thessaly, and the ruler of the wind.
Only he can give this to you.
And the angel amazons who killed Hercules smiled
and were jealous of this gift, for they too wanted
the neverending pain of lust and love
to hang between their legs like trophies on a wall.

Temptation (excerpt from a novel)

We all have heard stories about the innocent-hearted people who have tampered with the unknown, and unknowingly unlocked the door to secrets that lead them to the dark side. They find themselves trapped in a world of temptation, demons and witches. This is one of those stories.

The year was 1950. The place a small town in rural Georgia. It was a hot dusty day in late July, so hot the birds were not flying in the sky. The pigs the family kept in pens lay motionless in the mudholes they had rooted to keep cool. School was out for the summer. The kids did not have much to do but play games and practical jokes on each other. Or they could learn to hunt and fish— skills that would be with them throughout their lives—or look for wild berries in the fields.

Three kids in this family of sixteen, most of whom had no relation to one another, were watching the second to youngest, a boy named Lou who was about ten. Erlene, about thirteen, said to her brother Homer, who was two years older, "You see, Homer? I told you that boy is crazy."

June Bug, who was sixteen and no relation to the other two, said, "Shhh. Quiet, Erlene, he might hear you."

They peeked around the corner of the two room shack they lived in with the old woman they called Mom. The shack always leaned to the right.

"What is he doing now?" asked Homer.

"He's just settin' down behind that old fig tree," said Erlene, "talking to his self and looking down yonder in them there woods. I'm going to tell Mom."

"You ain't going to do no such thing," said Homer. "Let's go see what he's talking about."

"You know that boy can't *talk*," said June Bug. "It takes him half an hour to say hello, he stutters so bad. You can't understand what he is saying."

"I don't care," said Erlene. "I want to know what he's talking about."

They walked over to where Lou was sitting behind the fig tree. He did not hear them coming. He was in a trance-like state— humming and tapping his feet, rocking his head from side to side, and looking off into the woods. When the kids got right up on him, Erlene touched him on the right shoulder. It stopped him, made him jump. He fell off the rock he'd been sitting on and looked up at them. The sun was in his eyes. They were rocking from side to side in the back of his head, like he was coming out of a deep sleep.

He said, "Da-da-da-don't d-d-d-d-do-o-o-o that. Wh-wh-what y-y-you t-t-trying t-to do, s-s-scare me to-o-o-o d-d-death?"

The boys laughed at him trying to talk.

Erlene hit Homer in the back.

"I'm going to tell Mom. She told you about laughing at him! Now quit it!" She bent down to help Lou up. "Are you all right? What are you doing behind this old fig tree, talking to yourself? People going to think you're crazy, and them white people are going to come and take you away."

"I-I-I ain't c-c-c-crazy! Y-y-y-you d-d-d-don't hear th-th-that m-music d-d-d-own th-th-there?"

"Music!" Homer said. "Ain't nothing down there but old pine and oak trees. What's that smell? Smells like something has died down there."

"It does smell like something has died," said June Bug. "Ain't no buzzards flying around. You know if something had died, them buzzards would be the first thing you'd see."

"I don't smell it no more," said Erlene. "Probably nothing but the wind."

"It's so damn hot," said June Bug.

"Hush your mouth, boy. I'm going to tell Mom you be cursing!"

The days passed. Lou's strange behavior toward the woods about a half mile away became more and more frequent. He was seen getting closer to the edge of the woods, sitting in the tall grass, humming and rocking his head from side to side. His grandma saw him one day sitting among the tall grasses.

She called out the back door. "Lou! Lou! Get back here to this house, boy! There are snakes in that grass out there!"

The boy did not hear her.

The old woman became alarmed, and called for two of the older boys in the house, Clifford and Snap. The boys came running.

"You boys go down and get that boy out of the grass before a snake bites him!"

The boys grabbed big sticks before going down to the field. As they got closer, Snap said, "Damn, it stinks down here! What's that smell?"

"I don't know," said Clifford. "Let's just get that fool and get out of this grass!"

When they were right up on him, they called out, "Lou! Lou! You hear me, boy?"

As Snap, Lou's brother, raised his hand to hit him in the head and get his attention, a cold chill ran through him. It made him hold back his hand from striking the boy, as though someone had hit him and taken all the baseness out of him. He spun around holding the stick like he was ready to kill something, but there was nothing there. He looked at Clifford.

"Grab that boy, and let's get out of here."

Each grabbing an arm they picked him up and started back to the house.

"Put me down! Put me down!"

They ignored his cries, though he fought with everything in him to get free.

The old woman was watching them with both hands on her hips. They brought the boy to her, and dropped him at her feet.

"I didn't tell you to drag him up here. You could have hurt him."

"But Mom, we was scared there's something wrong with him," said Snap.

"You was scared? You boys go out hunting hogs all night long, and you're going to tell me you are scared there might be snakes in the grass out there?"

"Not the snakes, Mom," said Clifford. "It's the boy. Something just ain't right with him."

Lou looked up at them from the ground. The woman reached down and grabbed him by the hand.

"Get off that ground, baby, and go out there to that spigot and wash yourself off."

The touch of the old woman's hand was so soothing to the young boy. He looked at her and smiled and hugged her around the neck. Then he went to the spigot to clean himself off.

On Sunday, two days later, Ms. Rosalie, the kids' grandmom was dressing herself in her Sunday outfit. She was going visiting in Somoney, the nearby village. She was a tall goodlooking brown skinned woman with a strong frame. When the kids were at school, a man or two from the village would come by to lust for her love, and be groomed by her strong touch. As she walked out of the house into the yard, she saw the kids playing a game they called Jump-board.

They would get a log from a tree, about four feet long and fifteen inches in diameter, and put an eight foot long board in the center across it. One of the kids would stand on one end of the board, and another at the other end. The one in the air would jump up and come down as hard as he could, propelling the other kid into the air. He in turn would come down, sending his partner up, and this would go on until someone fell off the board.

The old woman called out, "Kids, I'm going to Somoney to see someone. I will be right back. Charles Junior, look out for the kids while I'm gone."

Charles Junior was the oldest. He was nineteen, a big dark skinned kid. Everyone liked him because he was a well-mannered young man.

"Where is Lou?" asked the old woman.

"He was just standing right here," someone said.

"Find him now," she said.

"Aww, Mom," all the kids seemed to say at the same time.

"Hush up and go find him. He might be under the house with that dog. Go look and see."

All the kids went to different sides of the house, or shack. It had been made of wood cut from the nearby trees, and placed on big rocks to keep it off the ground. The kids knew if they called for Lou he would not come, so they called the dog. His name was Whitey. They knew the dog would give his whereabouts away by barking.

"Here, Whitey! Here, Whitey!"

The dog started barking.

"Come here, boy," said one kid. "Here he is!"

The dog came out wagging his tail.

"Lou, come out of there!" cried one of the kids.

No answer.

The old woman said someone had to go under the house and get him. The girls knew they were not going, so the boys started to look around at one another.

"Charles Junior said, "Unh unh, I'm too big to crawl under there." He looked at Bull who was nine, almost ten.

"All right, I'll go, but I better not get no fleas on me."

Bull started crawling under the house. It was dark, hot, and dusty. Spider webs hung from every corner he looked into as he crawled inch by inch under the house. The smell of stale air from rotten bones, the dog, and the old wood from the house made him hold his breath when he moved, and breathe in his shirt when he stopped. As he came closer to where the dog had come from, he called out, "Lou, Lou," but no answer. He kept going.

Someone from the outside called, "Do you see him?"

"No!" He crawled farther, squinting his eyes to look all around, until he spotted Lou. He was laying in a pit he had rooted out in the ground. He was laying among old cat, dog, and chicken bones, and what looked like old rotten opossum, rabbits and crows hanging from the beams of the house. Bull crawled into the pit with Lou. It was about five feet around and three feet deep. Lou was laying with his face in an old rag. His knees were tucked underneath him, his hands were over his ears, like he was trying to block out the sound of the outside world. Bull could hear him humming a chant of some kind. He reached out and grabbed Lou's hand. Slowly and gently he held it in his own.

The humming stopped. Lou turned to Bull. His eyes were red like fire and shining like a cat's. Snot was hanging from his nose. Foam-like saliva was around his mouth. The look in his eyes frightened Bull, but he knew he had to bring him out. So he took the inside of his shirt up around the neck, and very carefully cleaned his nose and mouth, all the while talking to him.

"Come on, man, Mom is waiting for you. She has some sweet potato and sugar cane for you." That might get Lou's attention, so he'd not give Bull a hard time getting him out. Bull knew he liked sweet potato and sugar cane.

Bull crawled out of the hole backwards without letting go of Lou's hand, looking him in the face and smiling all the way out. The first thing everybody outside saw was Bull's face coming from under the house.

The old woman said nervously, "Where is he?"

"Right here," Bull replied. He came out still holding Lou's hand, and then Lou came out.

The old woman reached down and grabbed the boy by the hand. "Come here, child. Are you all right? Lou, you're going to be the death of me if you keep this up!" She called Erlene and Keeter. "Go get me the foot tub and put some water in it."

Laverne started brushing the dust off Lou as the girls brought back the water. Nobody noticed Bull go into the house, where he kept his personal belongings. He looked inside an old Prince Albert can and took out a half dollar coin. He put the coin in his pocket, and ran back out over to the fence alongside the house. On the other side was a field where the white farmer up the road lived in the big white house, a remnant from the times of slavery.

He kept his cows— black angus cows, about ten of them. They were big tall cows. The young bulls in the herd would chase the kids whenever they came into the field. The kids would play a game with the young bulls; they would wait until the cows got down into the woods about a mile away, then they would run across the short side of the field. Now the cows saw the boy running across the field, but it was too hot for them to move.

The girls put the tub behind an old homemade quilt that was hanging across two lines nailed to the house. It was where the kids washed up in the summer. They did not have running water in the house. Still holding the boy's hand, the old woman led him to the tub of water. While she washed his face she started to sing.

"Will the circle be unbroken by and by, Lord, by and by.
There's a better home awaitin' in the sky, Lord, in the sky."

The boy liked to hear her sing. It made him feel good and relaxed, and then he could smile not only with his mouth, but with his eyes.

"Lou, what's wrong? Why are you acting like this?"

He looked at her and raised both shoulders, as if to say he didn't know.

"Erlene said that you said you hear music."

"Yes, Mama."

"Coming from them woods?"

"Yes, Mama."

"What kind of music?"

"I don't know."

"You don't know what you are listening to?"

"No, Mama. It's just in my ear."

"In your ear?"

"Yes, Mama."

"That just don't make sense."

Then the blanket was pulled back and Bull came in breathing hard, like he had had a long run. The old woman looked at him and started

39

washing his face, too. He had a small bag in his hand that he put on the ground. The old woman sent for clean clothes for them both. When they got dressed the old woman grabbed them by the hand and started toward the village.

On the road the two boys pulled away from her and began to play. Bull still had the small brown bag, which he opened. Inside were two pieces of sugar cane and two small potatoes. The old woman looked at him and smiled. She knew how he had gotten Lou from under the house. He just made good on it.

Ahmad Rashid

The Humble / Attitude / Exclamation

I have never wrote a poem
that I could say was mine.
I write in the hand of the unheard
sarcophagus on Potter's Field.
Living in the mumbles of
drunken people who tell truths,
while at times my
pen lies proclaiming
my existence in a literary Bop
Where I drags slightly
the right foot,
and flex the left elbow.

I have never wrote a poem
about shit I'm not vaguely familiar with
So I write for empty stomachs,
and felony beefs.
The meaning of me and we
are in the spirit of each word,
spoken or otherwise.
I write.

I have never wrote a poem
that I could say was
sprinkled with flowers and grasshoppers.
They're cool, but I don't
write for them,
I write for
those who know

suffering. For those that
have been betrayed by this world.
And I write for
those dreams
that never were.

The ideas that pace prison
yards, and the screams
throughout Hell begging to
be expressed.
In heaven.
On Earth!?

I have never wrote a poem
that was actually mine.
I write for
insecure
white boys and their tunnel
vision of horror.
I write for
victims of legal lynching,
and modern day fugitive
slave laws.

When I write I feel
close to myself.
The gods within laugh and
play happily together.

I write so I
can never be lied to.
Even though I never owned
a word,

every now and then I
steal a few, and change
people's views.
I even write poems for
preachers Imams and Rabbis,
who be jivin' with
dogma, and killing divinity.

I wrote the Holy Ghost,
and she wrote me back,
told me how her baby father don't
pay child support.

So I wrote him a poem.

I have never wrote a poem that could
be considered classical or
compatible with Western ideas.
My shit is sacrilegious
perversion, with a
neo-revolutionary slant.
My poems have fist fights
with punch lines, and
do back flips on
dirty mattresses.
And have forced love
out of women
in my mother's bedroom.

Still and all
I have never wrote a poem
that I could say was mine.
The best poems

are the ones which have yet to
be expressed.
So I keep on writing,
hoping I might levitate
while doing so.
Nothing is impossible in a poem,
that's why I burned a few
and gave the ashes to the Jinn.
Spoken or otherwise
I have never wrote a poem
that I could say
was mine.

Israel Fernandez

There Beneath The Canopy of A Full Moon

Sitting on the edge of a cliff
overlooking the valley,
I reached up, grabbed the moon,
and smoked it!

A rush of adrenaline
surged within me.
A smile grew on my face,
until it met at the back of my head.

Samadhi?
Nah! I don't think so,
But there beneath the canopy of a full moon
I took a shortcut to Nirvana.

Crude Awakening

As I drew the cup to my lips
To take a sip of tea,
The reason for my quest became clear
I saw the reflection of me.

I am my own worst enemy.

Monkey Mind

My thoughts are racing a mile a minute. I am reminded of the last words
      I heard my Roshi speak before I left for Attica: "We must
      learn to tame
Our monkey minds." As if that were an easy task for this dreamer of
      dreams. Dreamer of Dreams? I just thought of a name for a Doo
      Wop group, if I were to start one. I'd call it "Dizzy Izzy and the
      Dreamers."
Now that's a cool-sounding name! If only I
Knew how to Sing, Sing, Sing (With A Swing). Ah! The Benny Goodman
      Band. Now that was Jazz—Swing Jazz, that is.
Every time I hear that music, I'm taken to another place and time. I just close
      my eyes and within minutes I am drifting away. "When you find
Yourself drifting off, bring yourself back to the counting of the breaths.
      This way we become the

Masters of our own minds. You must tame the mind.
It must
Not be allowed to tame you." All right, all right, Roshi, please.
Do me a favor. Get out of my mind and let "me" learn to tame the
      monkey.

Trapped

An entire china set in pieces on the kitchen floor.
What is going on?

Judgmental eyes peer down upon me. The unspoken words:
What a Klutz!

Hot flashes, embarrassment, anger, confusion.
What is happening to me?!

A dirty suit, lost time, questions thrown at me from every direction:
"Who are you?" "Where do you live?" "Can you remember anything?"

No. Wait! Yes, it's all coming back.
Curse the alienation, this burden on my shoulders!

No key unlocks the door.
Freedom is a bittersweet dream.

I want to be free to do the things I love; I want to be the best person
I can be, but I am trapped.

Envy, Pain, Isolation, Limitation, Exasperation,
Paralysis, Suffering, Yearning, Epilepsy.

Twenty Company Thirteen Cell

To this miserable life, I will not surrender
And exist only as a ward of the state.
I refuse to allow myself to be programmed and rendered
An ordinary house pet. That is not my fate.

I proclaim my birthright, right here where I stand.
I am first a human being and an individual as well.
I have a soul; a spirit; I am a man;
Not an animal, as you say, to be locked up in a cell.
And yet, for now, this prison is where I live.
So it is here that I carry out my bid.
Still, I'm working to make things right; giving what I can give;
Paying the restitution for the things that I did.
  And it **is** my vow to make things right—long before I'm set free
  Because I owe it first to myself, then the public, and, of course
                    my loved-ones who are waiting for me.

47

If Only He Knew

Iron cast bars and forty foot walls encase me.
A hawk rides the wind toward the setting sun.

Within the confines of my cell I sit in meditation—
The moon, the evening's chandelier.

Shades of green flood my eyes—green grass, green trees,
state greens. A cat scurries across the yard.

Behind these walls names are replaced by numbers,
And they say, "The key to freedom lies within."

An officer once said to me, "You belong to the state!"
But there's a cliff atop the hill overlooking the valley.

He said to me, "Once you're in, you can never go back!"
If only he knew how many times I've left.

Butterfly

Daydreaming,
I saw you riding
a butterfly called love.
As you fluttered across my mind,
the wind whispered into my ear
that your destination was
a place in my heart.
Tailing you was a poem.
Its beginning,
a starburst
its ending
a sight unseen.

A Life!

Deep within a concrete cage
with bars that cast shadows
as strong as steel,
I came of age
In a place where the fool is king,
and the bird's song causes pain,
I watched the world grow through
windows made of smoke and mirrors.

Night's Wintery Darkness

In the grasp of winter's darkness,
tiny white crystalline stars,
none ever exactly alike,
slowly descend

Spinning as though I'm on a carousel,
I stare into a motionless sky.
Using the tip of my tongue and
the palms of my hands,
I try to catch as many as I can

Tiny stars
tingly to the taste and
soft and chilling to the touch
turn to liquid dreams.
Where dreams fade
crude realities take their place

A wind
as menacing as a child's nightmare
and emotional as a sadistic lover
pursues and confronts from all angles
giving the stars
a sharpness like a stiletto

Avoiding the sting
to face and hands
my eyes are slits
as I bow my head
and wrap my arms tightly around me
in the grasp of winter's darkness.

A Season

December wind,
sun sitting low on a ridge,
geese fly south.

The Projects

Yelling,
the patter of feet,
tag, you're it.

Neighbor

Same routine,
banging, stomping, whistling, singing—,
shutthefuckup.

The Noise

Bang! Clang! Bang! Clink!
and there were other noises
I could not describe.
I sprang to my feet seeking
the origin of my tormentor,
the noise.

From my window
nothing
but a bright summer day, and
Bang! Clang! Bang! Clink!

The noise was bouncing off
the walls of my cell
trying to push its way into my head.
When pushed — I pushed back.
It began to fade
as sleep descended.

The dawn of a new day
took me to the window,
I needed to know
what had been occurring in my world.

The noise was gone.
Amazingly
earth had been moved.
Many colors greeted me.
Flowers where the concrete had been
danced to the urging of a gentle wind.

Waiting

Grains of sand slowly trickling down an hourglass
are the sheep of my dreams,
they hurdle barriers and deposit me
in places I desire to be.

An image becomes tangible in the pit of my stomach,
the gestation period seems to last an eternity.
Will I ever give birth to my dreams?

And how many Christmas Eves do you have each year?
As you wait
for night to turn to day
for day to turn to night.

Parole Officers' Seminar

I zoned out for the moment
and zoned into a not-so-distant past:

Ms. Spam is talking about deeds.
Quote, "You know what you did!
And don't play yourself!
You know what you plan on doing!"
(Emphasis hers.)

Ms. Spam looks at Mr. Fry
who starts talking about rules.
Quote, "They're held to a set of rules
that you can never see—!
Of course you can appeal their ruling!

(Emphasis his.)

What the fuck is going on here!?
(Emphasis mine.)

Ms. Spam and Mr. Fry collectively start talking.
Quote. "Nothing says you're guaranteed anything!
Now shape up and handle whatever!"
(Emphasis theirs.)

"Will someone please tell me
what the fuck is going on here!?"
In the zone I realize
stupidity rules.
Emphatically so!!!

Warring Gods

When Gods make war in their temple
men, seeing and hearing them,
act as vermin,
falling into ditches.
I, who am man and not made of this stuff,
feel angry,
and would rather die cruising in sin,
a death most fitting to insult the Gods.

At night when the warriors sang,
I found myself in a southern bed
wounded from a lunch of love.
I thought I was dying,
and it wasn't fear
but love that sent me to the Gods.

An early death in the night for me,
and to die on my knees?
That song is unsung.
I am not damned to travel a long
maddening road.
Fate has other plans for me.

When the Gods made war and sang
in their temple,
I found myself intoxicated
from the night's hot wind.

Is It Just Is

When the lights
go out
I greet a strange
and wonderful friend
then break it with a lit match
for I am afraid
of what I do not understand.

The Poem

The Poem
Is the hand in motion
To the zipper of your skin
Onward opening
The bones
Of your soul
Setting marrow free.

Amanda's Visit

Amanda, my daughter
came to see me today
ten years ago she went away
because of arrest and things I won't say
      people vicious, cruel just like me
      people vicious, cruel not like me
      against small children

I remember the baby smile
seven years old
when I touched and kissed her cheek
now she's grown beautiful and bold

She came to visit me today
prison walls cold and wet,
but her smile and tender hand made me flesh and blood
she came to visit and gave me fragments of ten years
we seemed new and strangers
words were slow and excited
the excitement could be heard
even without words
and in my heart the marching band sounded
I wanted to hug her, hold her
tell her, "I miss you, I miss you, I love you,"
and I ached all over, thinking of the passage of time
hearing her speak, the passage slipped away
but passage of time burns day by day
year by year, burning memories, thought, desires
and even hope and bonding between her and me
bonding between her and me
all the lonely nights, laughless days, endless suffering
from alienation, hatred, boxed cage, monsters fighting
fighting monsters in my head, in my head wanting suicide
and I didn't want her to know
how vulnerable her smile made me.

Allen Alim Santiago

Rays of Sunshine

Ray of sunshine, brighten my day you do, giving life
to the dark spots within.
Ray of sunshine, so small yet so powerful. Warmth
casting a glow so tender.
I wake up to you when you're there, and think of you
when you're not.
Longing for your presence.
I pity the blind and unknowing,
they are unaware of your beauty
and the abundance of happiness you cast
upon the seeing.
I know you're not forever, yet your glow will remain.
Ray of sunshine,
no rain, hail, sleet, snow, tornado, nor volcano
can keep my thoughts or your soft radiant
rays from shining through.

Big Strong Hands

Thirty-six weeks of construction. My time is near.
Oh yeah, it's here.
Clean my face, clear my lungs, a resounding wail.
My presence welcomed.
Vision blurred, figure misty, but I know it's him.
Big strong hands handle me ever so gently, with care.
I am hungry, I let it be known.
Sure enough those big strong hands feed me.
My first words identify him.
I know, for his smile tells me so.
Eager to learn, learn I do.
I see him over there, paying no mind.
See me? No? Guess I'll have to force you to.
Look, no hands!
Whoops of laughter, big strong hands clapping,
I'm center of attention.
Warm gentle knowing hands.
Something amiss.
Where are those big strong hands
I know exist?

A Silent Song

I woke to the early morning silence.
Gone was the musical chatter of the sparrows
and the throaty cooing of the pigeons perched
on the bars outside of my cell.

The sun filtering through dust-covered windows
served as a Stonehenge timepiece casting its shadow
on perfectly aligned steel bars.

Imprisoned I felt. Bars in front of me,
bars behind me. Trapped in a space barely big
enough to move around in.

Lured by a beckoning blue sky and picturesque
mountains, with trees standing tall like steeples
marking home, so inviting, open and free,

I watched as she flew into the invisible screen.
Trapped and imprisoned by its confines,
desperate was her attempt to escape. Afraid,
terrified, wings frantically flapping.
Trying to reach the small opening at
the top and the promise of freedom.

I watched as she hung her head in despair
and defeat, accepting her imprisoned fate.
I whispered, "Don't give up," as she sat
staring at home.

Gone was the early morning chatter
and the soft cooing
Revealed in the eerie silence was why
jailbirds don't sing.

The Ride Home

As the bus sped down the open highway and into the city,
the smells, sights, and sounds of the metropolis seemed to
flood my mind and my senses with long forgotten memories.

As the bus rolled past the familiar landmark of Yankee Stadium,
I could almost hear the roar of the crowd and the sound of the
ball echoing off the bat as the home team rallied in the
bottom of the ninth. I almost cried out, "Newspapers here, get your
nightly newspaper here!"— a long forgotten song of my youth.

As we crossed the bridge leaving the Bronx, the polluted
smell of the Hudson River reminded me of the time I had to
choose between the river or jail. I could still feel
the waves smacking me in the face as I desperately tried
to stay afloat and out of jail.

I wonder if this is a ride home, or a ride back to the
steel front doors.

It Started In America

It started with slavery in America. Bondage.
The black male beaten, shackled, and stripped.
A war between the states where the Blacks were the stakes.

A prize won for a job so well done that
it cannot be undone.

It started with the end of slavery in America.
Bondage in another form. Done so well that you
can hardly tell.
Can you look behind these prison walls
and tell me that slavery is gone?

Slavery is wrong in any form, so how can you
ask me what's wrong? You are scared of me because
I am Black. Because you are always thinking I'll
strike back.

You show a smile of hope and a frown of despair
and build new prisons with a scornful stare.
This is America you see, but not what America
was meant to be. The land of the free.

One look behind these walls will tell it all.
Slavery in America is still going strong.

On the Road of Life

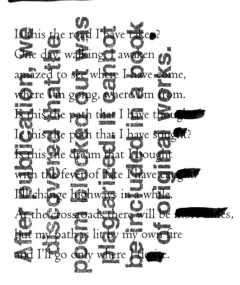

Is this the road I have taken?
One day, walking I awaken
amazed to see where I have come,
where I'm going, where I'm from.
Is this the path that I have thought
Is this the path that I have sought?
Is this the dream that I thought
with the fever of fate I have caught?
I'll change highways in a while.
At the crossroads there will be more miles,
but my path is lit by my own fire
and I'll go only where I desire.

After publication, we discovered that the poem blocked out was plagiarized. It can not be included in book of original works.

The Bars

Tall tin soldiers,
the long afternoon shadows of barred windows
slowly lean across the cramped quarters
of my inside world.

Tipping closer
with each setting degree of the sun,
they bid Good Afternoon
without really meaning it—
just another group of nosy bastards
in a world full of more of the same.

But this time of the year,
the bars put up a formidable façade,
masquerading as great howling wolves
amid their own amplified wall reflections.

My sink and toilet,
a convict's personal friends
among the world of innate objects,
resent the bars' rigid military posturing;
I've heard them refer to the bars as "the watchers."

It is true they never tire
of watching me watch the world
just outside the block windows,
even now as I observe the courtyard between cell blocks,
the September hair atop this small tuft
of the earth's great round scalp

slowly lengthens and lays down
in softly graying green-brown anticipation
of winter's great white wrecking ball.
The bars would hide all this from me if they could.

I'd lay down now but this afternoon
my pillow is stuffed with that change-of-season mixture
of dreams and desires,
memories and nightmares,
the rapidly cloying vines
that can squeeze your temples,
stifle your breathing,
and twist you in two different directions,
like listening to Oldies and waiting for parole.

I'll sit here instead,
back turned to the bars;
my books in their shelves,
a hundred taxis lined up on Eighth
in front of the Garden on Fight Night;
I'll hop in one,
and as the Printed Word sets the mirrors
and puts its outstretched arm
across the back of the front seat,
"Where will it be, pal?"
I know the bars will recede
further and further from my view.

Letter To A Friend

Have you been following me around
or have I been following you around?
I probably first encountered you in some school book
or class film or encyclopedia—some tool of education,
but I can't remember now anyway.
I recall first hearing your name: *polar bear*,
and my vision of you then
as a kind of giant, white, fluffy dog,
with all the mystery of ice and snow
and northern stars
hidden somewhere deep within you.

I know your name cannot be *polar bear*;
you know your name, whatever it is.

When I first saw you in the flesh,
you were a captive of New York City's Central Park Zoo.
You were locked in an outdoor cage
too small for both your body and your dignity.
You weren't white or fluffy;
your pelt was greasy, matted and discolored
like a discarded bathmat in an old gas station.
You paced nervously, rhythmically,
always exactly the same amount of steps
forward and back,
all the while repeating bizarre head-swooping ritualistic motions.
Over and over again.
Always exactly the same.
Your eyes did not acknowledge me,
but instead saw through me
or past me
or beyond me.
Perhaps you didn't even see me at all.

Since then, I've learned the meaning of *driven to distraction.*

Since then, I heard they remodeled that zoo
and even designed state-of-the-art, cooler, larger,
more humane cages for you and your friends.
You in particular were mentioned
and I was glad to hear this.

Since then, National Geographic has kept me reasonably informed:
the guy in Alaska who was convinced
he was about to lose his sled dog
to a large, menacing polar bear.
Instead, the dog signaled the universal sign for play time
and the bear signaled his agreement,
and together they romped around and mugged for the camera.
If I ever encounter you in the wild
I'll try like hell to remember that sign.

I saw you again on a television special;
you sniffed the Arctic summer air.
You appeared electrified, hungry, free;
I felt that way one time
when I was on the run,
three thousand miles from home
and down to my last five dollar bill.
Since then, I'm neither hungry nor free.

Since then, I encountered a Zen teacher
who told me the chance of a soul
being incarnated into human form again is the same
as a sea turtle poking its head to the surface of the ocean
and emerging in the center of a floating life preserver.

Since then, I've thought both of seeing you and of *being* you.
Since then, I've also spent time in a cage too small.

Mark "9 Box" Benyo

My Father

Always on the edge.
His ways, his life, his job.
My mom and us kids.
All of us.
I seen him cry twice. When he slammed my mom's hand in the car
door,
and when his brother Terry died.
I wanted so badly to reach out, but didn't know how.
Lost in the confusion of me.
Running across the cornfield
in back of the house,
the rain hitting the ground,
like my tears on this paper.
Perfection was the rule of all days, every day.
And I was always the unperfect one,
trying so hard to please the man I love so much,
failing miserably time and time again.
I couldn't even hear his beat, much less
march to the drummer he wanted me to.
And then I'd feel the other beat
as my brothers and sister would beg him to stop,
and pull him off me.
Taking his frustrations out on my imperfections.
Feeling rage I didn't understand then and still don't now
at the one who had done it all for me:
scouts, baseball teams, jobs, provider extraordinaire,
self-made man.
Whose only failure was the imperfect son.
Home was fear and fear was home.

Left when I was 12, never returned or ever looked back.
Scared for my mother, my brothers, and my baby sister.
Now my whole life has been one series of prisons or another.
After the last 11 year stretch inside these walls that are
just like home
I tried to go home again, though I heard it couldn't be done,
but only for a visit
To pay my respects, confront my past, face my fears.
I ask myself how I can hold my ground against enraged psychopaths
intent on my demise,
Steel flashing all around,
like moonlight on blood puddles,
But tremble at the thought of a 95 pound man and our past.
I seen him last Easter in '94, and asked him straight up
what he wanted from me,
As anything I could give was his to have.
My braid was 16 inches long and I loved my hair, but he told me
behind every horse's tail is a horse's ass,
and that's what he wanted.
I cut it off with a pair of scissors and handed it to him.
He hung it on the mantle of his fireplace.
Glad it wasn't my balls, or was it?
He's dying now, his cancer is eating up the one that put so much
fear in my heart.
My regrets nibbling my soul
for the sad shell of whom is my old man,
who can still call the shots on me.
It never changes, does it?
His upcoming death
as in his life
still has me
on the edge.

Under The Harvest Moon

Well it's hard, so hard, so very hard, to live in this world full
of gloom, as I sit here each day with decades to pay,
under the Harvest Moon.
It's the middle of another sleepless night, my family expected me
soon, cause I am still young, though I can no longer run,
under the Harvest Moon.

You feel the fear that surrounds you here, trapped inside this tomb
under the brightest stars, these walls and these bars,
under the Harvest Moon.

Harvest Moon in here, out there
Harvest Moon shining everywhere
Harvest Moon, better feel it, or you're doomed,
Harvest Moon.

My brothers in here, well I hold them near, as I try and write
this tune, to say it in verse, that it could always be worse,
under the Harvest Moon.
It's near the end, and I am waiting, my friend, to leave this
world full of doom. You wait with me, as we long to be free,
under the Harvest Moon.

—*Mark "9 Box" Benyo and Oscar Berrios*

Michael P McLean

Little Cans

A little boy is standing, frozen by his eyes.

His mind is cloudy like a storm due sky,
his vision's clear as a settled glass of water. Why?

His heart knows the reason; understanding escapes him.

Odor invades his nose like termites storm a house,
unwelcome guests.

A stench cloud in the air, little boy is still confused. Why?

Speak, little boy. "Ma."
Still cloudy, still confused, vision becoming glossy
as tears fill his eyes. Why?
Eyes too full, leaking warm tears down innocent cheeks,
splashing to the floor.

The boy draws near to what is dear to him,
heart bleeding, mind frazzled.
Reaching for her hand, he says it. "Mom? Mom?"
I love you etched in his heart.

Little boy pulls her hand.
A toil in vain.
He tries, he cries, she won't get up.
The little cans have slain her, she's stuck there
for the night, a captive to the floor.

Tomorrow she won't remember, won't know he stood nearby.
Tomorrow she'll buy more little cans,
and kiss the floor once more.
Why?

The little boy grows up, he is tall and strong and tough.
Inside the man a boy is standing, with his mother nearby.
Except now he knows why.

It's the little cans.

My Love

To touch you, a gift to my soul.
To have my fingers brush across your soft tender skin
is a dream that I yearn to come true.
My ears itch to hear the sweet harmony of your voice,
to listen to the gentle beat of your heart,
while softly nestled in your bosom.
Your absence pains my entire embodiment,
I thirst for your presence.
My day, my life, revolves around my devotion to you, to us.
You fill my every thought, giving my life deeper meaning.
Without you I am a puzzle with the last piece missing.
With you I am whole, an unexplainable completeness envelops me.
Life without you is not life at all.
An immense void would engulf me should your love, your being
escape my touch,
my mind, my soul, I LOVE YOU.
Not only your physical being, your outer shell,
but the deepest extremities of your soul, the real you.
Every bit of the vast depths of your essence...YOU.

The pages of time turn slow for me, so torturously slow for me.
Without you near me an emptiness swells inside me.
I am but a book, a sad book, paused on the outskirts of a deserted life.
Just a closed book collecting lonely dust waiting for you.
Praying for you to rescue me from the shelf of despair and
abandonment.
Open the pages of my life again, so the breath of life and love flows
through my veins, fill me once more with unspeakable joy.
I wait for you, long for you; my patience knows no bounds.
You are my love, Crystal.

Snowing

Oh great, it's snowing.
Snows falling like white feathers after a pillow fight,
gently blanketing the city.
I sip mocha-mint coffee, dipping a hot
glazed croissant in a cafe on the edge of nowhere.
Just a place called the Village,
amongst the concrete commotion.
I sip & dip while snow falls, covering
city grime, city slime, but I'm not blind.
I see what the snow can't cover, can't change.
A street beggar to you, a bum, a
homeless person. To me?
A human being breathing the same air
and wondering why things aren't fair.
Snow falls. He dips into a can,
his only plan for the day,
perhaps the next day, too.
Sky's still leaking snowflakes, no wind,
just peaceful flakes falling to a hard ground,

an even harder world. It's my second cup,
a snow carpet has rolled out over sidewalks & grime.
Yes, the grime is still there, though I don't see it.
I pretend it's not, like I pretend he's not,
but he is, still looking for who knows what.
I hope he finds what he wants, what he needs.
I need to thank him for helping me see,
he doesn't know it but I found me!
Yeah, I'll thank him
after my next cup.
Then I'll go home and kiss my wife like I used to.
I'll even pet the dog
and let him eat from the table just this once.
The snowfall started it, and that man at the trash-can finished it.
He said so much without saying a word.

Jewel Presley

Izar (To hoist, haul up, heave)

Why must I   dig?
You want to look deep inside
Peeling away the layers of time
To find the haze of destruction?
You want to hear the echoes
From the vibrations of pain?
Do you have to flow inside my arteries
To gaze upon the walls
To see the life that once was, or the
Residue of illusions

Why must I remove scabs layered deeper
Than the lava from a hundred volcanoes
Excavating lost cities full of towers of pain
Traveling subways of endless massacres
Flowing rivers
Of constant chaos;
Streets paved with worthless wisdom

You want to dig for the artifact of misery
Civilizations of distrust;
Who are you to walk the halls of my mind
Ride the spirit of my dreams
Inhaling the dust of my reality to
Experience the recessed places of the unknown?

Can't you see the continent of buried lives
That could have been?

Must I rip open the membrane to the soul
Where you feel the aura?
The desire?
Seeing the flame of burning brightness
That could melt the window to your soul?
Searing heat of power that grasps your mind

Like talons of a great falcon;
Tasting the salt of dreams
Smelling a world on fire

Must you know   why
I cry in my   sleep?

Sun

Always calling me sun
With the glowing smile on his face
That's my boy, listen to your mother
Sit down be still. Put your
Head in the window.
I like Dad's new car
Sunshining, windrushing, cows.
What's that smell? Horses
Cool man wearing fly hats
Veteran of the war and
The scars to prove it, it looks like a quarter moon.
I know he had to be tough to have
A scar like that and live.
White uniforms with red patches, hot nights
I was in my mother's belly
Wait for the car to stop, before you open that door!

Listen to your mother!
Don't bring that stuff in the house.
Why you talking to my father like that?
Get out the window before you fall.

Mother

Like the waters of the sea
Whose depth is measured by the courage of your heart,
Like the waves constantly crashing on the shore
Wearing rock to sand.

The tree whose roots are firmly planted
Powerful enough to sustain the body,
Protective of the essence inside.
Firm but able to bend with the change of seasons.
Never too firm to bend with the wind.

The wind whose caress is soft, subtle, smooth
A gentle force
Holding back destruction.

The fire in your eyes, the sparkle dim
Yet hot enough to melt the doubt
  Celadon   Fragile
      Smooth
      Strong
      Beautiful.

Like It Was

Ghetto used to mean together
A haven of protection, a big family
Someplace to hide when you're on the run
An open door for a warm meal
A hard floor to sleep on

The winos were harmless, sleeping on the doorstep
Somebody's son, brother, father who needed
A place to stay, on a sunny day they would carry
Your groceries for a nickel, a rainy day it cost a
Dime, now crack cost too much
Now they sleep on the curbs, people call them
Homeless, dispossessed, tough love

Broken glass was used to keep 5-0 off the street
So you could swim in the pool the fire hydrant made
You ever see 5-0 change a flat tire?
Today the streets are covered in glass vials
And dirty needles

Back when the street light came on, children
Were in the house under the covers safe
Because young black boys were fair game, hunted
But you wouldn't see their face on the
Dry milk box with the government rations

Now they take little girls so there won't
Be little boys anymore
Empty lots were playgrounds, camp sites
And wild life
The condos are now subsidized for the movers

And uppers

Mother's day came twice a month, so did Mr. Skippy
And the Julep man, all the neighborhood kids
Lined up with their quarters and nickels
Now they line up with beepers and 9mm
No more penny candy, Now & Laters, Boston Baked Beans
Juju Bees. Your big brother's clothes you wore, hand
Me downs two sizes too big are Karl Kani
Nautica, Fubu made too big.

School was fun couldn't wait to go, now children
Are scared of metal detectors, security guards
Mama used to smile, hug and kiss
Today she cries
People loved to get together in the ghetto
Now ghetto means get out.

Sit Your Black Ass Down

Sit down for a minute, this is something
I should have done a long time ago
You have something to do, somewhere to go
Wait, just wait a minute.

Sit your black ass down.

Listen, hanging out isn't slick
Nothin' new, don't you have school tomorrow
Don't you know every time you walk out
That door you become a stereotype
Threat, criminal or stat

What do you have there, lift your shirt
Up, what I'm not your father
Where are you going?

Sit your black ass down.

What kind of gun is that a 9mm
Don't you think you are doing what
They want, you see me every day and
I carry a weapon, yeah I have one too
My mind is my 9, my thoughts are the clip
My tongue is the bullets and my smile will kill yah
The only black on black crime I knew was the
Black barrel in my face and the other figger behind the trigger
Lil' Bro, it's mental, not physical
What, your girl is waiting.

Sit your black ass down.

Girl, who, what are you doing with a girl
I know you're not making no babies
Do you know what a condom is
Safe sex is no sex
You still in school, living home, no job
Playa hatin', you think you a playa
You got game.

Sit your black ass down.

When I came up we didn't worry about
Losing our girl because we had something
To offer besides looks and fat pockets
We didn't change girls every week, we were

In it to win it, thinking about the family
And the future.

What, old man
Don't let the gray hair fool yah, make me school yah
Mentally blast yah, chronically crash yah dental
Verbally slash yah mental, the scars I leave are
Unseen, maybe mean but to get your attention
I will take you around the world mentally
Challenge your ability
Show how silly you'll be
If you don't listen to me.

Sit your black ass down.

Puffy is not a Bad Boy, he's a business man
Educated, graduated, H.S. and college
Don't you know it's a conspiracy to
Systematically take the money out of the black
Community every time you read a magazine
Watch TV, you are being programmed to
Commit a crime, where do you think you are
Going to get the money for a Rolex, Lexus
To impress, thugging, mugging, drugging.

Sit your black ass down.

Lil' Bro, I love yah
I'm sorry for not being there when you needed me
Hopefully you won't make the same mistakes I did
Never turn your back on your
People we will be great once again.

Herby Ehinger

On the Road

There it was.
Laying in front of the car,
lifting its head slightly.
Its body shaking while it attempted to move.
One eye fearfully looking at me.

And I looked back at it.

I wanted to heal it with my touch,
and carry it like a child
into a world where pain and suffering don't exist.

Instead I ran off nervously
looking for a murder weapon at the side of the road.
The driver of the car had already told me that he could not
do it,
so I pulled a road marker out of the ground
and ran back to the car.

The headlights were mercilessly shining on its head,
and I looked at it again:

the innocence,

the softness,

the beauty.

I saw no more fear, but only wisdom in its eyes.

I froze my emotions, closed my eyes,
and swung the instrument of death:
much too soft probably,

So I did it again
with more force and eyes wide open,
aiming at the skull,

until my weapon was red with blood,

and I was sure
that I had killed
not only the poor fawn,
but some part of my own.

Things I Didn't Know About Myself

Before I came to prison,
I didn't know how much other people's opinions meant to me.
Didn't know or want to know how I looked at myself
depended on how those same people judged my actions.
Back in the so-called free world it seemed so simple to say,
      "I don't care what anybody thinks of me.
      I just do what I want to do."
And I believed it, too.
Most people in here can't even admit that much to themselves.

I didn't know I have a habit of putting myself down whenever I get a
chance.

Didn't know it is better to feel pain
      than to feel nothing at all.

Didn't know I could be so cold and disinterested in other people's lives.
This place will teach you.
Didn't know my father could show feelings other than anger and
frustration, until he came to visit me. Didn't know how much I love
him; didn't know I was so much like him.

Didn't know my mind is a prison, tougher than the one I am living in.
Didn't know I am in charge of building and
destroying it.

Didn't know I would enjoy reading and writing poetry in my cell.
In front of a movie theater in Chicago I saw a red sign blinking on and
off: *Believe it or not!* Fascinated, I took a photo.
My German mind couldn't figure it out, but it felt as if it was a
mysterious message directed at me.

Now I am sitting in front of a jury, telling an incredible story

with a tired face. They chose not to believe me, but I gave them
all I could. Believe it or not.

I didn't know I could live without her.

Ode to My Cell

Four white stars on the ceiling
some naked girls on the wall
cardboard boxes packed with legal papers under my bed
books I read more than once and books I will never read
a locker full of food, just in case, but never locked
three pipes filled with steam in the winter:
a guaranteed nosebleed every morning

a window with a view of another cellblock; sound effects included
Fifty-four square feet

A box full of photographs from the past

Years ahead of me
self-destructive thoughts mingled with hope
and a flashlight searching for a movement of my body every hour
of each night

The singing of birds at 5:00 am.

The door is locked

waiting for the sound of keys

A fan, still unemployed, its head hanging low
plenty of postcard images from different worlds
a map of the world and one of Europe; I hardly ever
look at them any more

An extra pillowcase keeps me company during the night
you can't keep a secret from these walls
and cockroaches shall inherit the earth
silent screams of pleasure and pain
and prayers to an image of God I ceased to believe in years ago

And thoughts of her
mostly her

she appears like a goddess
on the bed, where I live, where I practice safe sex
like a teenager having discovered secret pleasures,

and always in fear of getting caught by his parents
a toilet bowl filled with dying sperm all trying to reach the sewer first

The rusty iron bars outside my window are so obvious;
sometimes I overlook them
and there are days I can't wait for the door to be locked again.

Lap 15,512

Again
we walk in circles
Our eyes focused on the concrete in front of us.

Sometimes I look up to see concrete walls, barbed wires, towers,
infrared cameras, and robots in uniforms – green, blue and gray.

They are shooting a movie again. Somebody is waving at the tower.
He wants to be in the picture.

I keep walking in circles.

Most of the times I even run. Only 20,988 laps before I will be
deported. I wonder if somebody keeps count. Can't trust them,
you know.

Look at this guy. He is walking in the opposite direction.
Doesn't he know he is increasing his sentence?

If I had any time to spare I would tell him.
If I had any time to spare I'd look up at the sky.
If I had any time to spare I'd look at their faces
                              and cry.

Unknown

Some unknown forces are pulling you down
you can't sleep
you awake in the middle of the night
crying your eyes out, crying and unwilling to believe
of course, it was only a dream—
only a dream?
A nightmare
and even inside it you refused to believe
that she had died

You play it over and over again
people are throwing her belongings away
you try to stop them
clinging to everything that once was hers
smelling her
and knowing she is alive
she must be alive

There is no evidence to prove her death
of course they are lying
of course you alone know the truth
you can always die, too
you are walking on death's slippery shower shoes

We were throwing each other kisses from a distance
in my dreams there always seemed to be
an obstacle between us
your lips were moving, but I didn't understand a word
I tried to tell you how beautiful your lips are
and you were smiling
the world at your finger tips.

Raindrops roll like tiny diamonds on concrete
and a blind man with a stick walks by
he too wears a watch.

How much longer can I tell myself there is a reason
for everything that happens in my life?
How much longer can I hold on to my dreams?

I am not afraid of my own heartbeat anymore.

#110

I was
talking to my
homey on the phone
late the other night.

I said, "Peace."
He said, "What's up, dog?"
"Maintaining. Just trying
to do my bid," I said.

After a long sigh
he said, "Damn, they got
my nigga locked down!"
I said, "Excuse me?"
"I said, I can't
believe they got my
nigga locked down."

At that moment
my third eye
generated a spark
and I flipped
like an acrobat—
I "spazzzed" out!

"Was Garvey your nigga?
Was Malcolm your nigga?
Was Diallo your nigga?!"
I shouted.

"Yo, son, chill...
Why you flippin', son?"

"And stop calling me son!"
I shouted. "I ain't your son,
unless you refer to the mental one
that illuminates the crevices of
your ignorance."

I said, "I be more
than that, black.
I be carbon, oxygen, nitrogen,
and phosphorus, physically,
be equipped with mental alchemy.
My funky phosphorus flows,
fondles your mind in the form of
adenosine triphosphate.
I be common to living cells.
I said, I be common to living cells.

I make up the part
of the chart that makes
possible the most complex
properties of all—
life and consciousness."

"Yo, you missed medication
or something?" he said.
"You straight trippin'!"

"Yeah, I'm trippin',
trippin' on a plane that
you can't even fathom.

I be the protons and
electrons that cause that
involuntary contraction of your
muscle groups: a burst of pure energy!
I be the dioxyribonucleic acid,
those chains that intertwine
and form patterns,
those chains that build
generations and nations!"

He said, "Dag, give a
black man a book
and he don't know how to act."

I said, "Tell me if I'm acting
as I transmutate, using the
principle of polarity for clarity.
Can't you see how me and my
chemical compound thugs kick it?
Creating consciousness
with vowel and consonants."

Not allowing him
to get a word in edge
wise, I continued,

"Can't you see how
Ahmad transmits thoughts,
transmits the word
from the nucleus of a cell,
unable to escape its membrane
for a fixed period of days.
Keep locked.

While I point poetic pistols
with no safeties at people
successfully squeezing the
chakras of suckers.
But that's over your head
and too deep."

He said, "You supposed to be my
nigga. You changing on me, dog."

"No, ain't nothing change,
it's just that the incubation cycle
of my third eye is complete,
and like June, 'I'm not no nigga!'
I be the isthmus that connects
the mental with the physical,
and the physical with the spiritual.
Nothing is stationary,
everything is moving.
I be number 110
on the periodic chart
of elements."

And with that there was
a loud banging
sound, as molecules
crashed with one another,
and their vibrations
changed.

I hung up
the phone
on the clone.

Mika`il DeVeaux

Time

When mom sent me to the World's Fair with a dollar
plus a spiced ham sandwich
that's when I made up my mind
I even lied about my age
that's how bad I wanted to be a player
I got fake documents to increase my chances
I wore hats to look older
but no one gave me a shot
I became more determined and
played in the little leagues
the minors and bitties while waiting to step up
I did the things I thought would get me noticed
I was going to be a player
I had the heart, the instincts
and with my moves, I made semi-pro
just a couple of steps beneath the big guns
real players
million dollar players
I knew them all
talked with them occasionally
got into a few spots
hung out
I think the pressure got to me because
making it big was everything
but I needed keys by the bunch if I was going to really step up
and I was trying to get it
I wanted the ice
I wanted to drip with it
be dip, ya know

the shines — the silks
I had my Cadillacs, but I wanted a Beamer and a Jag
right before I could stack bricks
body dropped
then prison
and my career ended
just like that

Witness

Hettie Jones, the ex-wife of Amiri, old Leroi Jones
I needed to take note of who this was
so looking back I'd remember the connection to Nap Nap
one of the oldest prisons in the State of New York
with its castle-like facade and pink rocks when you get up close
this ain't no movie set
no muthafuckin' video
but real prison shit with steel gates every forty yards
and razor wire even on the roof
and lock in and lock out and on the chow and shut the fuck up
on the count
lock it down

Yeah, Hettie was here
from the Lower East Side
reciting poetry
using James Baldwin to provoke me to witness
to witness what I see
to witness what I feel in captivity
the insight, how much I've been enlightened
and witness what
lifting up my scrotum and

opening my mouth for the jacks to search for contraband
witness spreading the cheeks of my ass during the ritual humiliation
witnessing what
a testimony of submission

I still got power
fuck that
I still live, unlike the others who get turned out and fucked
who get the drugs and disillusioned
and are made to die before they die
no suicide note in my cell
witness that
witness the fact that the steel has made me cry
witness the fact that I hurt
that I get scared in the middle of the night
standing alone
but I still love
witness that

Voices Under The Harvest Moon

Frank said never to believe everything you hear.
Who ever heard of a dog barking in falsetto?
Everyone talks of young love
but few ever say anything that makes sense.
Brother Charles certainly doesn't know.
He sent a letter of intention to a man.
I read it myself.
He made claims that black and white were imagined things and that
only gray was real.
Perhaps he's afraid of making choices,
taking sides.

Gray.
He's a fugitive now and being chased by real police.

Herby can't stop running.
That's lap 15,512 on the road that goes in circles.
He has to run.
He writes letters to roaches.
All right, I'll go for that, but the roaches answer back.
They didn't think much of the ode to his cell.
I wonder who else he writes.

James sang silent songs.
At the end of the concert he spoke.
Said he was never alone, that Diana, an extra-terrestrial,
was always with him.
My guess is that's why he sings silent songs.
When together they speak a language only they know.
I can't tell you everything about those two, but
the whole thing started in America
It's one of those long weird stories.

One thing though,
they'll never get back to where they came from.

Alejo knows how true this is.
He talks about the things he thinks of in his cell.
He found out ignorance of the law is no excuse too late.
That's why he talks in his cell.
In his cell? Which one?

Pity he can't get out or get in the cell he wants.
Now people are complaining about him!
They don't like that he talks in his sleep

They're tired of it and have made plans for a burial of all those pictures
that keep him up at night.
He talks to them, to the shadows.
He talks of yesterdays.
Yesterdays to which he wants to return but never will.
It's not romantic.

Jeff never came,
Probably for the best.
No one knows what's on his mind.
We heard rumors of his dead friend.
He still keeps him in that place.
We heard of his primordial screams from a time
no one but him remembers.

Ask Sonny.
Sonny just may have been there.
He is older than you think.
He wrote a letter to a friend that hints at recollections of freedom.
You remember freedom?
Sonny is a writer.
He writes letters to society sharing his wisdom.
If you ask me, he's writing to ask permission to explore a new found
territory called desire.

I wonder if they'll ever let him.
No one ever lets anyone.
He should stop asking and just go.
No one owns the land.

Janine came too.
She was different.
She sought to join the fight for the sake of fighting,

or was there some other motivation based on frustration.

There always seems to be a catch.
Still I listened.
She spoke harshly to the yous on the other side.
My eyebrows rose when she spoke of Huncke.

I thought she said Honkey trying to ease in that old revolutionary
stuff from the 60s.
She must have picked that up in Paris cruising the isles.
Which side are you on?
Now I'm asking the questions.
Gotta ask when the position is not clear.
Was that the mask or the face?

Cecil knows.
I'll ask Cecil about Janine.
Cecil likes to tell secrets.
Cecil told me that the gods were crazy.
I agreed, but I wonder who told him.
God one day, dog the next.
It's according to how you flip it.
Evil live, live evil. Get it?
He saw a corpse and said, "This ain't living."
Now that's wisdom!
I wonder how he can still think of traveling after all these years.
There's no place to go.
It's a wonder he can still see.
Actually, it's only been a short while.
Time is relative.
Cecil should stick to becoming a poet,
Becoming is what life is all about.

What You Don't See

When I turn to walk away
all that macho stuff don't mean a thing
I carry my heart back to its hiding place
wiping sweat brought on by the fear
that you will not return
not because you don't want to
but because you can't
bear another night of being alone
isolated and empty in an empty bed
when I turn I have to dab my eyes
so they won't see how swollen they are
with tears held back too long
tears so hot and heavy they want to roll like the river Jordan
tears fueled by hate and anger and love and emotions I can't describe
I don't understand walking away
having to leave you and all that is real
all that matters for distortions and perversion
for faking and pretending - for the insane, illness and demons in
chains behind locks and bars
I feel like I'm being eaten alive by insects
bitten and sucked
bit by bit, piece by piece
still I hope
hoping to emerge whole enough to hold you
to pillow your head when you need
when you need me, if you need me
the thinking makes me so afraid that I shall die
before our first vacation together
before going shopping with you at the mall
before our drive to your mother's
before being Daddy for real

before being Hubby and Grandpa
when I walk away
I hurt too

Not The Rhetoric

The next time you read one of your poems to me
Say something I need to hear
Something that will ring in my ears like a blast
Something that will cause my head to ache
Like you just knocked me out
But before you begin,
Swear to tell the truth
Act serious, don't smile and please
Promise not to serenade me
Let the birds do that
I need to be stirred
Stir me
I need to be inspired
So inspire me
I need to be lit on fire with your ideas
You got any ideas?
Then burn me
Burn me with that light
You got light?
And what have you seen?
A vision?
Something mind blowing?
What have you heard?
Something fresh?
Then share that
Say something that will make a difference in my life

Something that will help me to fight
I am a fighter
Are you a fighter?
I am a warrior
Are you a warrior?
We are at war
Where are the war words?
Where are the fighting words?
Where are all those roll up your sleeve words?
Those get down words
Those we down, going out together words
Those words that call all hands to get dirty
Give me something to create with
Something to build with
Don't leave me like you met me
Feed me
Give me a little something to excite my taste buds
Something nourishing
Just a little something to get my thing right
Something to hold me until tomorrow
Something I can use to deal with what I got to deal with
Like my foxhole during the day
Like my concrete bunker at night
And look at me when you speak
I'm trying to create an atmosphere where I can live
Can I live?
And if I speak the truth to you
Then speak the truth when speaking to me
Don't try to entertain me with your poetry
Arm me with your words
Make me mo' dangerous
The next time you read one of your poems to me

Alejo Dao`ud Rodriguez

Sing Sing Sits Up The River

How alive,
the rhythm that waves move at,
it's as though they're breathing,
in and out,
like seasons change, nature
itself inhales and exhales a spirit
that air too breathes
almost human and kind,

how the wind comes to visit me,
blowing past curls of razor wire.
Rows & rows of it—razors
wrapped around the top of electronically juiced fences
intended to shock
until they kill.
Yet the wind still has not abandoned our visits,
even after having been cut a million times,
the wind bleeds, we become blood brothers

How humane & touching
That the bars feel the openness,
the freedom outside, the space beyond
the other side of where I stand—Upstate New York.
Where underground railroads once ran & ran
cold, tired, & hungry in the night
but can't stop
gotta keep movin'
gotta get to a Black freedom
where now prisons are built in the hills,

how thoughtful.

How sparrows still remind me there's a spirit
free. And that it breathes.
Even where winters are the coldest
& holidays are just a thing from another life.
Even in this cold that burns,
the sun still kisses my forehead
as if I were as pure
as a day breastfeeding in my mother's arms.

How unimaginable,
how freedom comes alive
touching the sun
between bars.

Renaissance

Please. Don't preach to me.
I don't want to hear about religion.
And it's not even a question of faith, if I believe.
It's just the way that I've been colored.
The way a cell colors me closed in.
Colors me in so many shades of estranged,
that if religion is not freeing,
if it does not celebrate me too, then
I really don't have any use for it.

If ancient scriptures don't have anything to do with today
other than pacifying and subduing revolution,
if words can't jump out of books alive
and spell LIBERATION!
Then I don't want to read them.

Let amerikan dreamers read of religion
for themselves—into prison.
I'm already inside one.
I'm not trying to create another prison
inside me—inside prison?

The struggle is great enough
when it burns and rolls and presses like iron,
my soul, the sword that cuts
splitting faith beyond consciousness
and there's nothing there

And what images do you have
when you think of God? What prayers?
What comes to mind when you think of
never coming back to this life again?
What kind of bed for eternity?
What can you leave your children that can't be sold?

Do you question the color of God then?
Question God's sex?

Or is there a greater sense of connectedness
to that thing in your heart that moves?

Now tell me,
what do prayers say?
Do they touch as delicate as a baby, as afraid?
Are they as intense as nightmares, as chilling?
Because if we're going to talk about religion
then this is the gospel I want to hear about,
the return, the re-naming of souls.
Because this is the beginning of change.

Chicago, March 26...In a storm of fists and feet, Lenord Clark [thirteen years old] was beaten into a coma by a pack of white teenagers as he rode his bicycle last Friday on the edge of Bridgeport...According to the police, the teenagers later bragged about keeping blacks out of the neighborhood. The New York Times (printed March 27, 1997)

1997: The Rebirth of Segregation in The North

Lenord, did you know you made the New York Times?
No, it wasn't exactly the front page,
Hilary and Chelsea Clinton were there,
something about them on a safari in Africa.
And you, a young black boy
from a Chicago neighborhood
in the back on page 18A. I guess
the racist beating of a thirteen year old boy
who's now trapped in a tunnel of darkness,
a coma, isn't news enough compared to
the First Family's vacation in Africa.

Good Will Delegates preaching good will to Africans,
the beating of an African American boy into a coma,
this is more than a prophetic reoccurrence,
this is integration—double jeopardy—and
it's really scary how blind the people still are
to politics and promises to foreign countries
of blessings from a divine Democracy,
as though integration were working.
Promises that have yet to be fulfilled
in the U.S. of America:
you have just experienced what Human Rights
means to a black boy, Lenord.
The Human Rights that Democracy so proudly preaches
is no more than the toll booth where they collected kicks

to your head as payment, before they drove you into that tunnel,
that passageway, that bottomless pit of unconsciousness,
the darkness,
Democracy, Lenord.
But you're only thirteen.
Could I really expect you to know the irony
of what a Capitalist Democracy really means?
It's an illusion, an oxymoron, a social cannibalistic religion
without the totem pole, a modern cult

That drinks the blood of human sacrifices:
the blood of thirteen year old black boys and
the blood of Third World countries and
the blood of gray crack babies
shaking and screaming for just one last blast.
Was it the sound of their cries you heard echoing
in the darkness, Lenord? Or was sound
impossible to hear over the bombing going on
on black churches exploding in your head
in every beating blow beyond consciousness?

Did you try to fight back, Lenord?
Did you try to run? You must've at least tried to run, man!
Because they said that only your leg shows movement,
that it's an unconscious reaction to the pain,
but that's what they're writing about you, Lenord.
I hate to think of what's really going on in the darkness,
is the beating not yet over?
Are you still running further and further
into that tunnel of darkness?
Past Yusuf Hawkins and Emmet Till,
past countless faceless faces of black men

hanging from the trees.
Past crying slave girls lifting their blood-drenched hands
from torn vaginas? What about Tawana Brawley?
Does the darkness speak of what really happened
to Ennis Cosby?

You see, a black man is a black man is a nigger still
in this country. The Dred Scott decision has yet to be repealed.
Second class rights are the Human Rights afforded to African
Americans
by law, Lenord.

No matter how many Martin Luther Kings get assassinated,
no matter how many Michael Jordans play for the Bulls,
no matter how many talk shows Oprah Winfrey rates #1,
no matter how many colors Jesse Jackson adds to his rainbow.

.

The reality of the races is what has you in that coma
and it's as clear as black and white.
It's a reality that many wish would just go away,
but the reality is that it won't be changed without actively
being a part of your life and every other child's life
that you are sacred,
to be loved, nurtured, raised, and protected.

The Burial

He awoke before dawn
while the world slept
and unfastened his mask.

Then he began searching

for a mirror, lost
at the little boy staring back at him,
so curious, so familiar, so unknown.

The mask had been cracked
and it left an impression on his cheek.
The same place marked,
the little boy wears a scar.

Anger and hurt are in the younger's eyes,
he doesn't have the know-how
just knows it must be done.
The older holds the mask in contemplation
he knows it can't be fixed.

The graveyard sign read:
FOR MASKS ONLY
One by one—men come
mourning, crying, alone.
There are no tombstone markings
just a shovel
and a playground across the street.
Like the masks they carry
each man knows his own place
digs his own hole
and one by one
across the street—so many boys,
the playground comes alive.

Cecil Boatswain

On Becoming A Poet

You don't make a whole lot of money doing it.
Well, most don't anyway.
You must prepare yourself for torture
When you finally decide to do it,
Giving up everything you never really had
And the digging begins.
Now you are totally ready to suffer for what
You know or what others have told you.
Start by peeling away the scab, reopening the wound.
Poets must be able to do this over and over again
And blame no one for their misery.
They have even been called lovers of pain.
They are the ones who volunteer to sit quietly
In the electric chair,
Burn at the stake,
Be hung while the public watches,
Beheaded by their lover's guillotine
But they must do it!
Start with the simplest things—
A pencil and a blank sheet of paper,
Naked thoughts, and the desire to vomit up
Your entire guts on this piece of paper,
Then look at it with a vulture's eye.
You'll shed tears in the back of your mind,
Because it burns deep inside;
You'll fight for every bit of life you have left,
All in the name of poetry.
But whenever you decide to become a poet,
You will realize that it helps to
Ease the pain when you write it down.

My Father's Dying

My father is already dead.
He just lays there,
bedridden, motionless.
Mother,
she waits patiently for
Azrael to keep his promise.

In pain my father smiles;
he never learned how to cry.
The gloss in my mother's eyes
forms a single teardrop and
falls cruelly on my father's forehead,
echoing as it splashes into different
directions,
but my father's gaze and smile
are fixed upon the dark moth that wildly
circles the light bulb overhead.

Mother passes her hand over his forehead,
feeling the permanence of his wrinkles,
softly kissing him,
cupping his mouth and nose with her hand,
watching them disappear.
"He looks more peaceful now," she says,
closing his eyes with her hand.

The Gods Must Be Crazy

Shiva, the I Ching is against you.
You cannot restore an altar
And offer the voices of lost souls.
Your temple is a vacant room without candles
And you have brought men without possibilities,
Filled with emptiness, and impure souls for rags.
You can never teach them to clean the altar!
They have nothing but what they have come with,
Yet you claim they are the yellow helmets,
The new sun rising.
Your temple is only a stage for the wicked,
And I go in and out to free the evil spirits.
My gift is the open door.

After All Those Years

After being punished
For ten, fifteen, twenty-five or more years
Do you think you can just leave?
Can you imagine anything more terrifying
Than walking through those gates without
Looking back at that great square wall
That kept you in all those years?
Punishing you and comforting you!
Punishing you and comforting you!
Do you think you will at least miss it?
That somehow, inside, you loved being here
Under the eagle's wings?
You ain't got to worry about a damn thing!
You ain't got to worry about a damn thing!

You're Amerikkka's greatest son,
The tooth mother's greatest capture.
She has taught you how to bend your knees,
Stand up curved back and mop her welcoming floors,
Given you paint to embellish her halls of terror,
More terrifying!
And you've been smiling all those years at her morbid green,
Her institutional colors, her slavery that fits you.
So do you think after all those years of being
Trained that you can just un-train yourself and leave?
That you can enjoy the wonderful colors you've only enjoyed
As a crayoning child, after all those years behind those
Gray walls? The monotony!
The Sunday pancakes, re-fried French toast and greasy chicken,

The Mondays you wished there were something edible,
The Tuesday Yakasobi, murder burgers
The Wednesday killer liver,
The Thursday everything from the last four days mixed
Together,

The Friday lumpy oatmeal and fluorescent Kool-Aid
The Saturday cold cuts you go down to the mess hall just
To look at,

The cycle begins again on Sunday;
And you've gone to the mess hall for every meal,
Didn't miss a single meal in all those years.
Now why do you think you that you can get used to real food?
Home cooking, a gourmet restaurant?
After you've only had seven minutes to eat
And an ulcer bigger than your heart?
After all those years you still think you can just leave?

Well, maybe, but even though you leave the prison
The prison will never leave you.

Why I Burn The Mountains Down

There are gutters where creatures live,
Where creatures die before reaching the banks,
Where those that reach the banks
Become lifetime drunkards from the muddy water,
Staggering in their new life,
Like wingless bees, realizing they cannot
Gather pollen without their wings.
Their defenses die
And they become fossils.

I look at the mountains
And burn them down every day with my eyes.
The animals, unable to bear the scorching heat,
Bury themselves in the earth and become rocks.
The birds hustle through the smoke
While their young perish

Don't blame me!
There are reasons why I enjoy
Watching the mountains burn,
And there are reasons why,
When my eyes stop dreaming,
The mountains appear again:
Because I cannot light the fire,
I cannot touch the trees,
I cannot scale the banks,
I am a wingless bee.

She Is A Foreign Language

She is standing in the middle of the
World waiting for the sun to rise
Through the trees in the open field.
There's quietness when you listen to a woman's heart,
When you listen to what she is made of—
Two million passages, the soundless unison,
Like the nights in September when a rose
And a woman are one.
If you separate the stars from the moon
She will learn to be alone again,
Darker than the forest, cold from the blackness
Around her.

A Plane Ride Out of Captivity Into Freedom,
For Alejo

Lift off,
High-rises sway to the music of mechanical wings,
Eyes swoop down like an eagle's cleating claws,
As structures below fade under their own shadows,
Disappearing into the white mist of oblivious clouds.
For a moment I am attached to the empty space,
For a moment I am huge wings flying into freedom
Out of captivity, out of pain—
And my mind falls into a whisper of lost words,
As faces descend upon my conscience, painting pictures
Of sorrow, pictures of souls trapped inside
Walls thousands of miles beneath my unchained feet,
Beneath my thought.
I can feel their names gyrating upon my tongue—

Mika'il, Alejo, Jalil, June, Donkor.
I spit them out into the open air, into freedom,
So that their arms are spread, like birds willing to
Fly to unheard places, breaching all sense of time;
Now maybe time will not mean anything.
Maybe time will not be as consuming as a vacuum of silent
Imagination, waiting in the corner of disbelief and prayer,
Waiting to grab innocence out of experience,
And I laugh, a laugh of privacy, only to listen to its
Decay, its mockery, through the plane's echoing sound.
I disappear again into reveries of back home, into the
Descent upon this forgotten land, over seas and oceans,
Mountains, trees I will soon touch with my own hands.
I could actually taste the sweetness of my returning.
I am a child's eyes now, catapulting this adult body through
Memories that shake my mind like thunder. It is thunder I
Feel, as legs pushing out of the giant bee tease the runway,
And I realize that I'm finally home,
I'm finally home.

Produced at The Print Center, Inc., 225 Varick St., New York, NY 10014, a non-profit facility for literary and arts-related publications. (212) 206-8465